THE RIGHT DEGREE FOR ME

The RIGHT DEGREE FOR ME™

WHAT DEGREE DO I NEED TO PURSUE A CAREER IN EDUCATION?

JOSEPH KAMPFF

ROSEN PUBLISHING®

Published in 2015 by The Rosen Publishing Group, Inc.
29 East 21st Street, New York, NY 10010

First Edition

Library of Congress Cataloging-in-Publication Data

Kampff, Joseph.
What degree do I need to pursue a career in education?/Joseph Kampff.
     pages cm.—(The right degree for me)
Includes bibliographical references and index.
ISBN 978-1-4777-7873-9 (library bound)
1. Education—Vocational guidance—United States—Juvenile literature.
2. Teaching—Vocational guidance—United States—Juvenile literature. I.
Title.
LB1775.2.K36 2015
371.4'25—dc23

2014007487

Manufactured in the United States of America

Additional content contributed by Greg Clinton

CONTENTS

INTRODUCTION

Choosing to pursue a career in education can be one of the most rewarding decisions you'll ever make. Most people want to work in education because their own outstanding teachers, librarians, or guidance counselors have made a deep and lasting impression on them. They want to influence others in the same way. Future elementary school teachers may love working with children and want to help them learn the ABCs, times tables, and the life cycles of plants and animals. People with more specialized interests may want to focus on a single subject, such as math or writing, and teach students in middle and high schools. Librarians are as important as classroom teachers. They are the custodians of information, making sure that the information essential to learning is well ordered and accessible to all students and teachers. Guidance counselors play many important roles ranging from helping students apply to high schools and colleges to coping with emotional issues or problems in school or at home. They also work with teachers and administrators to ensure that the students' needs are met. You probably know a teacher, librarian, or guidance counselor you admire and want to emulate. This book will show you how to get there.

A career in education is an outstanding way to make an investment in the future of individuals, communities, and the world.

What Degree Do I Need to Pursue a Career in Education? provides a wealth of information about the various degree programs available for prospective teachers, librarians, and guidance counselors. In addition, it includes information about teaching careers that you might not have considered, such working in higher education as a university professor, and teaching subjects such as art, music, physical education, and foreign languages. Because career opportunities in the field of education are vast and varied, this book also provides information on degree programs for working with special-needs students and in health services, in school administration, and in local and federal government making decisions about educational policy.

To be inspired to pursue a career in education is a fantastic start. That initial inspiration will likely stay with you as you earn your degree and going forward in the day-to-day trenches of your job in education. However, as essential as inspiration is, it can also be pretty vague. For example, a seemingly decisive statement such as "I want to be librarian" actually opens up all kinds of other questions such as: What kind of librarian do you want to be? Will you become a teacher-librarian or a research librarian? Do you want to work in an elementary school, high school, university, or public library? Are you interested in training students to do digital research, or do you want to work with rare manuscripts, microfilm, or other media?

Education is a huge field, and "a career in education" can refer to many different professions in teaching, counseling, health services, libraries, administration, and government. These professions include a wide variety of jobs. The more precisely you can envision and state what your career goal is, the more likely you'll be to attain the job you want most. By helping you narrow your focus and pointing you toward the right path to your desired career, this book will help make your dream job a reality.

CHAPTER ONE

From ABCs to Shakespeare

Who are your favorite teachers? Who have your favorite teachers been in the past? What do you remember most about them? Nearly all of us encounter at least one teacher at some point during our education who is inspiring, challenging, and changes the way we think about the world and ourselves. Teaching, in other words, is more than just assigning homework and giving tests—it is a profession the purpose of which is to help people (young and old) achieve their potential. This mission begins with very young children—known in education as "early childhood"—and goes on to include older children, adolescents, young adults, and adults. Teaching spans the range from children learning their ABCs to young adults mastering Shakespeare; from counting to ten to the most advanced calculus; and from writing one's name to designing a working spaceship. If you want to get involved in this amazing, dynamic, and difficult profession, read on!

Early Childhood Teachers

"Early childhood" (or "EC") refers to students who are between the ages of birth and eight, according to the National Association for the Education of Young Children. These are some of the most dynamic and exciting learning years of a person's life. Brain development happens at a rapid-fire pace, language skills are developing, and the foundations for basic social interactions are established. EC professionals are experts in the social, cognitive, and emotional development of very young children, and they use that knowledge to help their students strengthen the skills and attitudes they'll need as they grow older.

Of all the possible teaching professions, EC teaching requires a specific type of person: someone who truly enjoys working with young children. EC teachers use imaginative play, games, dance, and music, as well as creative problem-solving techniques to guide children to acquire greater intellectual independence and social ability. It can be exhausting to work with small children all day long, but with the right training and experience, it can be massively rewarding as well. Effective early childhood education can have long-lasting benefits, giving students the right start for success in school and in life.

If you are considering early childhood education as a career, there are several degree options and career tracks from which to choose. An associate of arts

Early childhood teachers help children develop social, emotional, physical, and academic skills through fun and engaging lessons, games, and activities.

(AA) in early childhood education is a two-year degree earned at a community college. A bachelor of arts (BA) is an undergraduate degree earned at a college or university. Programs that specialize in early childhood education usually take four years to complete. A master of arts (MA) in early childhood education is a graduate degree that requires two additional years of coursework. Some schools require their EC teachers to have an associate's degree in EC education, and others require a four-year bachelor of arts. If, however, you have a master's degree, you will have more experience, more knowledge, and probably a better chance of getting a job. To work in a public preschool, teachers must also have certification to teach in their state. The requirements for this vary by state, so visit the website for your state's department of education for more information.

Armed with a degree and a teaching certificate, the new EC teacher can work at a day care center, preschool, traditional kindergarten, Montessori school, or an elementary school. Day care centers are not academic institutions, which means that they focus mainly on childcare and socialization skills. Working at most day care centers requires only an associate's degree. Preschools are more structured and academic, and to work as a teacher in a preschool you will need either an associate's or a bachelor's degree. Teaching at the kindergarten level, when traditional "school" begins for students ages four to six, you may need a minimum of a bachelor of arts degree because the heavier emphasis on academics requires more specialized knowledge and experience.

TEACHERS TAKING TESTS? GETTING CERTIFIED WITH PRAXIS EXAMS

Getting certified to teach is not just a hoop to jump through on your way to becoming a teacher; it shows that you are intellectually prepared for the job. One of the main components of the process of getting certified to teach in many states (and U.S. territories such as Guam and Washington, D.C.) is to pass the Praxis exams. (Exceptions are Arizona, Florida, Illinois, and Massachusetts, where there are state-specific tests, so much of this information is still applicable, though there are differences in those states.) The Praxis tests are developed and distributed by the Educational Testing Service, the same company that creates the Scholastic Aptitude Test (SAT) and the Graduate Record Examinations (GRE). The purpose of the Praxis exams is to measure teachers' academic skills, professional knowledge, and subject-specific knowledge. Teachers who want to be certified must earn a score that their state says is the minimum; the "passing" mark is different in each state. There are three types of Praxis exams: Core Academic Skills for Educators, which measures skill at reading, writing and math; Pre-Professional Skills Test, which asks questions about how to be a teacher, what to do in the classroom and how to communicate with parents and colleagues; and the Subject Assessments, which are targeted at particular subjects like language arts or biology.

Montessori Means...

A Montessori school is a particular kind of early childhood learning center that follows the educational philosophy of the founder, a woman named Maria Montessori, who believed in experiential learning (learning by doing) and child-centered education (learning that is based on choices that the student makes, rather than directions given by the teacher). Montessori schools have their own intensive training programs to supplement the degree you already will hold.

Elementary School Teachers

In general, the complexity of working with students from grades two through five is higher than with

Elementary school teachers are experts in classroom management: using routines and schedules, one teacher can provide an education for a room full of students.

early childhood. As in EC, elementary school teachers are responsible for guiding their students through social, emotional, and intellectual challenges, but in these grades the challenges are more difficult and the stakes are higher. Elementary school teachers are patient, caring, observant, well organized, good writers and speakers, and have a deep knowledge of how children learn. These teachers are typically generalists, which means that they teach the same group of children a wide range of different subjects and skills, from science to poetry to waiting their turn to speak. Elementary school teachers have a deep knowledge of child psychology, child development, methods of counseling and

Social studies, reading and writing, math, and science are all taught in the elementary classroom, so elementary school teachers have to know many different subjects.

communication, and ways of teaching. This collection of knowledge is called "pedagogy," or the method and practice of teaching.

A standard elementary school class has between twelve and thirty students, each of whom will have different strengths and weaknesses. The teacher's job is to figure out what each student can do at the beginning of the year, and then guide each student to improve in those areas by the end of the year. This sounds fairly simple, but it is actually quite complex, so elementary school teachers keep careful records of student performance and progress, sometimes even day by day.

One student might be a strong reader but needs help with multiplication, and another might be a moderate reader but a whiz at division (so he'll need harder problems to stay challenged). Good teachers devise systems to evaluate their students periodically, and then differentiate the lessons so that every student is pushed to his or her potential and gets the right support along the way—all while having fun and loving school! The final important piece of the puzzle is communicating these results to parents and administrators in parent-teacher conferences and committee meetings.

Tools of the Trade

Teaching elementary school requires a bachelor of arts degree in elementary education and, if you plan to teach in the public school system, certification from the state where you work. This is a complex job, so a four-year degree is necessary. In addition, some states require teachers to earn a master's degree in either elementary education or another specialized area such as technology integration or reading instruction, both to boost their knowledge and experience.

Middle School and High School Teachers

Beginning in grade six, the general education found in elementary schools shifts to more specialized instruction, so secondary teachers—that is, middle school and high school teachers—must focus on a particular subject, such as math, literature, physical education, art, or history. In addition to knowing their subject, middle school and high school teachers must understand the special needs of adolescents and young adults. In college, these teachers take courses in psychology and classroom management. They learn how to motivate and engage their students, as well as how to assess their students for content understanding. These skills might sound technical, but teachers are well trained in how to run a classroom, how to prepare effective lessons, and how to grade students on what matters in their education. The best teachers make their jobs look easy. But don't be fooled. Teaching is a tough job that starts early in the morning preparing for classes and ends late at night, grading papers and getting ready for the following day. Teachers often bring work home to do on the weekends and holidays. That being said,

In middle and high school, teachers often assign independent projects and presentations to help students develop their research and performance skills.

teaching can be a lot of fun if you are well prepared and organized, plus you get more vacation time than people who work in the corporate world.

ALL THE SCHOOL'S A STAGE: A REFLECTION ON TEACHING BY THOMAS SNYDER

(Snyder teaches writing in the Genesis middle school program at Xaverian High School in Brooklyn, New York.)

Teaching is a performance art. Every day is a show that runs for six hours straight with a cast of hundreds.

The school day begins at 8:30, but I'm usually there an hour earlier. This is "me" time, when I prepare for the day ahead. I answer e-mails from students, parents, and administrators; review lesson plans to make sure I'm still happy with them (rewriting them if I'm not); and rehearse activities and objectives. This "backstage" work may seem minor, but solid preparation is instrumental to succeeding as a teacher.

The real performance begins with the first class. I've rehearsed the show a dozen times, but each class has

Thomas Snyder is seen here in one of the classrooms in which he teaches writing at Xaverian High School, in Brooklyn, New York.

about thirty variables at their desks with ideas about how the class is going to play out. When you design lessons to be student-centered, the students often steal the show. You'll have to make peace with this early in your career: Much of teaching is improv. The trick is to be flexible enough to incorporate these variables into "your" lesson.

Luckily, the first class is not the last time I'll teach the lesson. I deliver the same performance to other sections, refining the lesson each time so that the instructions are clearer, the transitions are smoother, and the work is better suited to each student.

I eventually arrive at a "free" period, although this is a misnomer. I usually spend this time grading so that the pile of work doesn't become too intimidating. It *will* become intimidating regardless, but grading during my free periods makes it *feel* otherwise.

When the 2:30 bell rings, the show is over. I like to stay for a while to put my classroom, which looks like a war zone, back in order. Organizing my papers lets me revisit the day and decide where I was successful and where I was not. Reflection, like preparation, is crucial for teaching well.

Leaving the building is the official end of the workday, but there is a solid chance I will do prep work at home: grading papers, researching lessons, and communicating with students. The show, as they say, must go on.

But Wait, There's More!

Secondary teachers aren't just involved in the class-room, however. Most teachers are asked to serve on school committees that tackle questions such as how much money to spend on computers or how to improve aspects of school life. Teachers can be asked to meet after hours to decide on a new

Working with older students means teachers need more specialized knowledge of their field. In the upper grades, teachers handle a single subject at an advanced level.

curriculum (what materials they will teach and how they will teach it), or they might be asked to serve as athletic coaches or direct a school play. If you are interested in a particular subject and want to understand it at a higher level, if you're very organized and motivated to always continue learning new things, and if you like to do extracurricular activities such as sports or theater, then teaching at the secondary level could be a great career for you.

Requirements for the Job

Secondary teachers need at least a bachelor of arts degree in their subject, but a bachelor's degree in *teaching* their subject, or a master's degree, is sometimes required as well. Teachers with a master's degree have spent more time and money preparing to be in the classroom and interact with colleagues, parents, and administrators, but they also have more experience and can be more successful over the long term. Administrators see a graduate degree as a sign of dedication to the profession, and it can boost your chance of landing a job. If you want to teach in public schools, you will also need to be certified by your state, which usually involves passing one or more standardized tests, writing short essays, a criminal background check, and other formalities. Check your state's department of education website for details about how to get certified.

CHAPTER TWO

Specializing

There are many options for people who want to teach. In addition to science, math, English, and history, you might consider teaching health and physical education, art, or music. These subjects are perfect choices for athletes, artists, and musicians who want to integrate performance and teaching. Another option is to teach special education, that is, working with students with a range of special needs. This particular career path requires exceptionally strong, patient, and dedicated people who have a passion for education and want to make sure that all students have access to the education to which they are entitled.

Physical Education, Music, and Art

It's often been said that those who can't do, teach. This statement not only ignores the fact that most people teach *because* that's exactly what they like to do, but it also overlooks the reality that people teach what they do all the time: Professional architects teach courses on architecture, business executives teach business courses, and practicing psychologists teach psychology in psychology departments... you get the idea. Physical education, music, and art teachers are in a great position to do what they teach at the same time. Physical education teachers are often as active as their students. They spend much of their time outdoors teaching kids the importance of a healthy lifestyle, the fundamentals of a variety of sports, and coaching teams in middle and high schools. Art teachers share their love of art with students while drawing, painting, or modeling clay. And in addition to introducing students to the history of music and teaching them to appreciate music and play instruments, music teachers often have the opportunity to play their own instruments, sing, and organize concerts.

Physical education teachers today emphasize overall physical fitness over sports, and they often teach health classes as well. This shift in focus was caused by concerns over the increase in overweight children and weight-related health problems

Teaching physical education is a fantastic way to promote fitness and teach kids to play the sports that you love.

in the United States. Students still play kickball, but as a physical education teacher, you'll also be responsible for teaching them proper stretching and cardiovascular exercises. You'll need at least a bachelor's degree in physical education and a state certification. You'll also probably need a certification to teach health in grades K–12. In health classes, you'll cover important topics such as mental and emotional health, nutrition, and drugs and alcohol.

Music teachers are usually required to have a bachelor's degree in music and a state teaching certificate. If you teach music in elementary school,

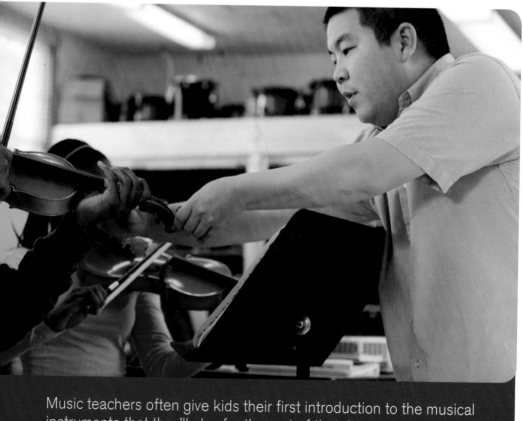

Music teachers often give kids their first introduction to the musical instruments that they'll play for the rest of their lives.

you'll likely teach general classes in all grades that introduce students to the fundamentals of music and playing simple instruments, such as the recorder. You might also be responsible for musical extracurricular activities, such as your school's chorus club. Middle and high school music teachers are more specialized. They teach rock and jazz band, chorus, and orchestra, as well as organize concert performances.

To be an art teacher, you'll need at least bachelor's degree and a teaching certificate that covers grades K–12. There are many bachelor's and master's degree programs in fine arts programs across the country in which you'll study the theory and practice of a specific medium, such as sculpture, oil painting, or photography. Art teachers in elementary schools introduce students to a variety of mediums and art movements. In middle schools and high schools, art classes are more specialized—you might focus only on pottery or photography in a class—and incorporate more information on specific artists and historical periods.

Art teachers often specialize in a particular medium, such as photography. This middle school photography teacher is working with students in a darkroom to select photos for a project.

TEACHING FOREIGN LANGUAGES AND ESL (ENGLISH AS A SECOND LANGUAGE)

With increased mobility, greater networking capacity, and a global economy, the world has become smaller, and the demand for foreign language teachers is on the rise in the United States. High-demand languages such as Arabic, Mandarin Chinese, Japanese, and Korean are taught in more American schools today than ever before. In addition, many schools are making foreign languages available to students at a much younger age. To teach a foreign language at any level, you must be fluent in the language and usually have a bachelor's degree, a state-issued teaching certificate, and be working toward a master's degree.

If you'd like a greater ability to move around than most teaching careers allow, teaching English as a Second Language (ESL) is a fantastic choice, as it's a great way for travelers to find work in other countries. Although it's not necessary to speak a language other than English to teach ESL, knowledge of your students' native languages and cultures will definitely help. There are many certificate programs in teaching ESL. They typically take one or two years to complete. The minimum qualifications for teaching ESL are usually a bachelor's degree and a certificate, but if you want to teach ESL in public schools or higher education, you'll need to have a master's degree in teaching ESL.

Plan B

It's always important to chase your dream, but you should also have a backup plan in case things don't work out. Teaching positions in physical education, art, and music are often the first to be cut during a school budget crisis. You might want to consider getting a second teaching certificate in a subject such as math or science just in case your job is cut. There is also the possibility of teaching art and music at private studios or working at a recreation center or a private sports facility. If you're an athlete, musician, or artist and think you might like a career in teaching, talk to your coaches and teachers to see what advice they have to offer. You should also look into the music, art, and athletic programs at the high schools and colleges in your area. It's never too early to plan for the future.

Teaching Students with Special Needs

Teaching special education can be one of the most challenging and emotionally demanding jobs in education. It can also be one of the most rewarding. Special

Teachers of students with special needs are specially trained to use many techniques and tools to ensure the right fit for their students.

education teachers typically work with elementary, middle school, and high school students with disabilities ranging from mild to moderate. As a special education teacher, you might work with students who have learning disabilities such as dyslexia (a developmental reading disorder), hearing or visual impairments, and autism. There is also a demand for people trained in special education outside of the school system, such as in hospitals and rehabilitation facilities.

Working with kids who need extra help to succeed in school means that a large part of your job will be to develop curricula and teaching strategies that meet each of your student's needs individually. All effective teachers must be flexible, constantly adapting their approach to the changing circumstances of the classroom. For special education teachers, this basic requirement is even more important. The best special education teachers are completely tuned in to their students' emotional states and behaviors while paying close attention to their social interactions. In addition to working closely with students, you'll be part of a large network of people—including parents, social workers, therapists, and counselors—working to ensure that your students get their educational needs met.

There are numerous master's degree programs leading to the required state certification to teach special education. Some programs lead to a general certification that qualifies you to teach special education at all grade levels. Other programs prepare you to specialize in a particular area, such as working with early childhood students with behavioral disorders or multiple disorders including deafness and blindness. Your coursework might include a class on teaching students with emotional disabilities, which looks at the social, genetic, and familial factors that contribute to emotional disabilities and investigates ways to promote positive social interactions. A more specialized course might focus on developing literacy acquisition skills for students with dyslexia.

Although special needs is usually associated with students with disabilities, gifted and talented students also have special educational requirements. Such students often challenge traditional approaches to education as much as students with disabilities. During your training in special education, you might take a course on gifted education that focuses on the major characteristics of gifted and talented students and the history and theory of gifted education.

See How the Pros Do It

Special education programs have a strong focus on integrating theory with practice. In addition to attending classes, students observe special education professionals in the field and participate in student teaching. Student teaching is enormously important. Becoming a teacher without teaching is a little like getting a driver's license without ever getting behind the wheel of a car. Different degree and certification programs have their own fieldwork requirements. But the best programs will make sure you get a lot of hands-on experience in the classroom working with a wide range of special needs students. This work will help you determine if you want to work in a specific area of special education. Specializing can help you in the job market. For example, there's been an increased demand in recent years for professionals—not only in schools—who are qualified to work with people on the autism spectrum.

If you think you might be interested in a career in special education, talk to the special education teachers in your school. Ask what made them want to pursue their career and what they think are the greatest challenges and rewards of working in the field. Their stories will help you figure out if teaching special education is the right choice for you.

CHAPTER THREE

Staying in It for the Long Haul: Teaching Higher Education

Teaching at the university level is definitely not for everybody. For one thing, there are relatively few university teaching positions. Universities usually have a tenure system in which teachers who have worked long enough, published enough books and articles, and have done certain administrative duties are offered a permanent position at the university. This is great for people who have found a tenure-track position, but it means that new job openings are fairly rare. This problem is made worse by the fact that there is no fast track to teaching college. Most teaching positions require the applicant to have

Working with adult students on the topics you care about most deeply is one of the joys of teaching higher education.

at least a master's degree in his or her subject, and many require a doctor of philosophy degree (Ph.D.). The average time it takes to get a doctor of philosophy degree in subjects such as English or history is more than nine years. But people who are truly passionate about learning and want to study and teach at the highest level shouldn't be discouraged. Teaching higher education can be a wonderful career choice. In addition to discussing the issues you care about most with other like-minded people and sharing your ideas in writing and at conferences, as a college professor you are in a position to have a profound affect on your students. Through them, you will help shape the world in important ways. This chapter will introduce you to the profession of teaching higher education and offer some pointers on how to get there.

PAYING THE BILLS

Most masters' programs do not offer funding to their students. This means you will likely have to pay for your master's degree yourself. The usual solution is to borrow student loans to pay for tuition, books, and housing. While it's often necessary, student loan debt can be a major problem for recent graduates earning entry-level salaries. Furthermore, you will be extremely busy in graduate school, and you probably won't have time to work a full-time job.

But a part-time position at the university can be a perfect way to make money while you're in school. What's more, your job on campus will look good on your résumé: Getting a master's in English? Work in the university writing center helping undergraduates polish their papers. Studying to be a teacher librarian? Get a job in the library. If your subject is math or foreign languages, work as a tutor. Talk to the department coordinator to find out what positions are available. Working at the university while you earn your graduate degree is an excellent way to get real-life experience at the job you want, as well as reducing the amount of student loan debt you'll have to pay back when you finish.

Working on campus as a tutor is a great way to make extra money while earning your degree.

Teaching at Community Colleges

Teaching at a community college is an excellent choice for people who want to work closely with students, many of whom come from underprivileged backgrounds. Class sizes are usually less than twenty-five students, giving you closer contact with your students than you would have at a four-year college. Community colleges typically offer two-year programs that award associate's degrees in arts, science, and applied science. An associate's of arts degree (AA) is for students who want to transfer to a four-year college and major in humanities subjects such as English, philosophy, or sociology. Associate of science (AS) degrees also transfer to upper-division college programs. These programs tend to focus on more specialized subjects, such as veterinary technology, environmental science, and early childhood education. The courses taken for an associate's degree satisfy the general education requirements for a bachelor's degree. (In fact, taking some of your general education courses at the local community college can be a good idea even if you're enrolled at a four-year college. Community college classes are less expensive than university courses. Just check with your advisor to be sure that the classes will count toward your four-year college's degree requirements.) An associate's degree in applied sciences (AAS), on the other hand, is a terminal degree. It trains students to work specific jobs in fields such as nursing, office operations, and automotive technology immediately after graduation.

In most cases, you will need at least a master's degree in your subject to teach at community college. The master's should be in your subject. There's no need to get a master's of teaching to teach in college, but you should try to acquire some teaching experience for your résumé. Ask your professors or department head if you can give a lecture or work as a teaching assistant (TA) or try to find work as a high school substitute teacher. In some cases, you can even get tenure at a community college with a master's degree. This is less likely if you live in a large city such as New York or Chicago, where there's a higher number of people with advanced degrees. In that case, you may be able to find work as an adjunct professor. Adjunct professors are part-time employees who teach at colleges and universities on an as-needed basis. Putting together a full workload as an adjunct means working at several colleges. Adjuncts are not part of the faculty of the college or university. They don't receive benefits such as health care and a retirement plan, and adjuncts earn much less than faculty members. On the other hand, adjunct professors are not required to do administrative tasks, which allows them to focus on teaching. Working as an adjunct may be ideal for people with master's degrees who want to teach higher education and have a flexible schedule. Faculty members at community colleges also tend to focus on teaching more than professors at four-year colleges and universities, but they also advise students, participate in new-faculty search committees, and sometimes serve as chair—or head—of the department.

Teaching at Four-Year Colleges and Universities

Teaching full-time at a four-year college or university is a completely different story than teaching at community college. Many of your classes will be held in large auditoriums with a hundred or more students. In a class this large, you will deliver lectures from a stage, having very little contact with your students. You'll have help from a squadron of teaching assistants who will grade papers and quizzes, write assessments, and give presentations that reiterate the material covered in the lectures. On the other hand, it depends on the size of the school: Courses at small liberal arts colleges tend to have much smaller classes than large universities. Although teaching well is important at four-year colleges and universities, your primary focus will be your

College professors often teach small classes in which discussion between students and teachers is actively encouraged.

own research and writing—at least in the years before you get tenure. Not only is the workload more demanding at this level, but also the competition for jobs is fiercer. You will have to balance research, writing, and publishing with teaching and administrative duties. The plus side is that you get to teach upper-level courses, which tend to have fewer students. You will also get to teach from your own research. Instead of teaching survey courses in post-1945 American Literature, you can teach a course that focuses on your specific interests—Toni Morrison's novels, for example.

The Long and Winding Road

For the best shot at finding a tenure-track job teaching at a four-year college or university, you will need to get a Ph.D. This means a major commitment to education. A Ph.D. is the most advanced degree you can get in many subjects. Ph.D. students go through many arduous years of study to be considered experts in their fields. When they're done, they're allowed to use the title "Doctor."

The track to the Ph.D. usually has three parts and can be finished in four to seven years, although it will often take longer. First you'll have two or three years of coursework, depending on whether you have a master's when you enter the program. If you don't have one, you can pick up an en-route master's. These courses will fill out any knowledge in your subject that you might be lacking and introduce you to the world of professional scholarship. Most programs require that you complete sixty course credits, but some will require more.

ADVANCED GRADUATE CERTIFICATES

It can be extremely hard to find a job teaching in colleges and universities. As mentioned earlier, the competition is quite intense, especially in large cities where there are many well-qualified people going for the same job. To increase your chances of landing a job, you can earn an advanced graduate certificate (or two) while getting your master's or Ph.D. Graduate certificates give you advanced knowledge in interdisciplinary subjects related to your own. For example, if you study American history, you may want to get a graduate certificate in women's and gender studies or africana studies, focusing on the histories, politics, and cultures of people originally from Africa. These certificates mean that in addition to teaching traditional American history courses, you are also able to teach courses on, for example, the history of American feminism or African American history. You will normally need to take fifteen credits (five classes) to earn a graduate certificate: two required courses and three electives. The required courses for a graduate certificate in women's studies might be Teaching Women's Studies and History of Feminism. The elective courses may be taken from a diverse range of subjects, including film studies, literature, history, politics, or art. Sometimes the courses you take for your graduate certificate will also count toward your master's or Ph.D. course requirements. Just make sure this is OK with your advisors. When it comes to course credit, assume nothing.

You will also have to pass exams. These exams can be oral, written, or both. They will test your knowledge and ability to make connections between different points within your subject. Finally, you will write and defend your doctoral dissertation. A dissertation is a long paper based on original research. It describes your own substantial contribution to the existing knowledge in your subject. This is often the most time-consuming part of getting a Ph.D. By the time you're finished, you are likely to know everything imaginable about your topic.

Many Ph.D. programs offer funding to their students in the form of a tuition waiver and living stipend. This is part of what makes certain Ph.D. programs so difficult to get into: Because they are funding their students, the number of students they

Ph.D. students spend a lot of time doing research. Learn to love your library and your librarians—you're going to spend a lot of time together.

can accept each year is limited. As a Ph.D. student, you'll earn your keep by working in the department. This scenario means that in addition to coursework, exams, and writing your dissertation, you will also teach your own courses or work as a teaching assistant. This work is extremely important. When it's time to look for a job, you'll be able to ask for excellent recommendation letters describing what an outstanding teacher you are.

While the road to a teaching career in higher education may be long, difficult, and uncertain, the life of a professor can be profoundly satisfying. If you set your sights on this goal, keep in mind the many challenges ahead and the strategies for successfully overcoming them.

CHAPTER FOUR

Information and Health Services

Great teaching and learning depends on a large network of people within the school. This chapter explores some of the many supporting roles at the faculty level of a school, including librarians, information specialists who understand curriculum, research, content management, and data analysis; health professionals who care for students' physical well-being; school psychologists who identify special student needs and work to address them; and counselors, those guides and mentors who help students make successful academic and life choices and transitions. Although these careers support the core activities of teaching and learning, each requires different certification, licensure, and degrees.

Librarians

Have you ever had a project to research and asked for help finding better sources than Wikipedia? Or browsed the fiction stacks for your favorite author or picked up a "New Arrival" book near the entrance to your school library? Librarians make all of these services possible. The library is the heart of a school or university. The most valuable educations—preparing students for life, work, and good citizenship—are built around reading, research, and writing. Librarians, particularly school librarians, are experts at information management, and this section explains the skills

Librarians help students learn about research, but they are also responsible for organizing and developing a school's research materials as well as managing a digital database of all the items.

a librarian needs, what the job involves, and what a library science degree offers.

School librarians need to be hyper-organized. They must love working with students and teachers to navigate the web of information available in books, magazines, journals, films, and on websites. Some librarians also manage certain school funds and the budgets necessary to purchase educational materials for the school or library. They then spend time cataloging those materials so that students can find them. Librarians will often meet with teachers at every grade level to better understand what projects and units are being taught and what books and online resources best support those activities. Is the sixth grade doing a unit on ancient Egypt? The librarian's job is to identify the best possible resources for learning about this important civilization—one of the world's first—and then go on to teach the students how to locate and use them. Librarians join professional networks to trade information, techniques, and knowledge about running effective and powerful libraries.

In addition to helping students learn how to research and collaborating with teachers to provide the best resources, more librarians are becoming computer and data specialists as well. This means that, at some of the best programs, part of training to become a librarian can involve working with large databases and data analysis, computer programming, web design and construction, and content management systems specialization. Most libraries run on a computerized catalog; before the 1990s, libraries had very few

LIBRARIANS: INFORMATION ARCHITECTS

You go to the library, search the catalog, find a book, and check it out. Easy, right? While the process of finding a book may seem simple, the actual system behind it is very complex. Because of the rapidly advancing technologies around networks and data, being a librarian is more than just knowing about books—it's knowing about digital media and databases. The founders of Google were interested in

Librarians are search experts.

the same problem as modern librarians are—how can technology help us find the things we are looking for, or introduce us to things we didn't even know we wanted to see? While Google indexes the entire Internet, library catalogs are special databases that contain indexes of library collections.

Librarians have had to expand their understanding of the digital world to provide the search services you might need for modern research. For example, how do you classify a video game or an app? How do you reference a TV show that is only available as a streaming video? How do you cite blogs and tweets in research projects? In retrospect, organizing a collection of books seems simple compared to designing systems of information that link books, news media, video, audio, and digital resources in an intricate web of connections. Being a librarian has never been so cutting-edge and exciting.

digital resources. To look up a book, you went to a card catalog, which was a huge set of drawers with cards in alphabetical and subject order. Now you just search on the library's website. Librarians are in charge of these data hubs, so they must update, maintain, and design them effectively. If you love computers, data, and information management, being a librarian might be just the job for you!

The typical librarian job requires a master of arts degree in library science. (Sometimes the name of this degree varies slightly, for example "master of arts degree in library and information sciences"). This is a graduate degree, so it assumes you already have a bachelor's degree in another subject. This degree usually takes two to three years to complete. Successful librarians are knowledgeable about many topics, so they can help a range of researchers, but they must also be technically inclined so that they can manage large amounts of data in a digital environment. A master's degree in library science qualifies you to work in university libraries, as well as a number of other jobs (not necessarily in a library) that deal with information analysis.

Counselors and Health Services

Physical and emotional well-being are as crucial to learning as are books and pencils. If a student is sick or worried, he or she can't learn effectively. Counselors and health care providers are responsible for addressing these important needs within the school community.

Keeping Students Healthy: The School Nurse

To address the most fundamental need—physical health—many schools employ a school nurse. Nurses who work at schools or colleges collaborate with

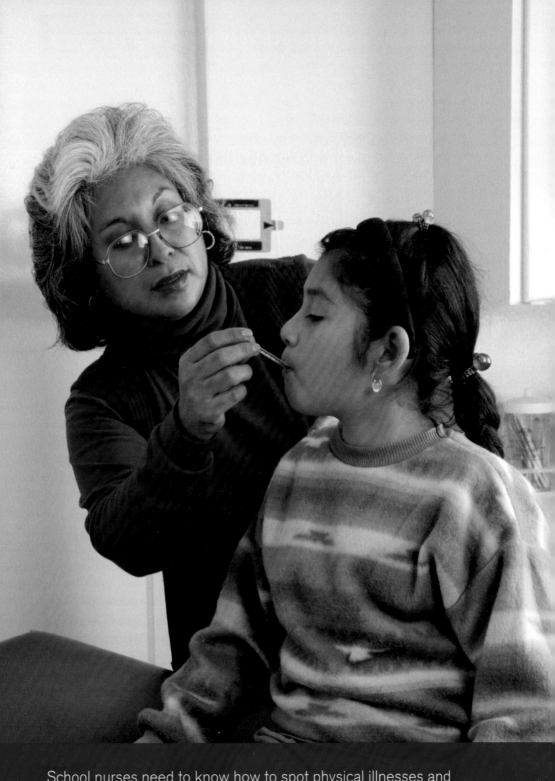

School nurses need to know how to spot physical illnesses and emotional difficulties.

teachers, administrators, and parents to support the health curriculum and increase access to health resources. They are the first line of defense for keeping the entire school community safe from infectious diseases. School nurses also respond to medical emergencies and provide first aid whenever necessary. Fewer than half of the schools in the United States have a dedicated, full-time nurse; most school nurses split their time between multiple schools. To become a school nurse, you must earn a four-year degree called a bachelor's of science in nursing, or BSN, and get certified as a registered nurse (RN). School nurses are familiar with pediatric medicine, mental health, and public health issues such as how to prevent and manage contagious illnesses.

A Shoulder to Lean On: The School Psychologist

While school nurses focus on the physical aspects of health, school psychologists and guidance counselors focus on students' mental, emotional, and social well-being. School psychologists are trained to work with individual students who may be feeling anxious, depressed, or are otherwise having trouble succeeding in school. They work with parents and teachers to pinpoint learning or emotional difficulties and design programs to help students manage them. Psychologists should be excellent communicators, empathetic (they understand how other people feel), and comfortable dealing with stressful situations. Becoming a school psychologist demands rigorous training. While some states require only a bachelor of arts degree in psychology supplemented with specific training in working with children, many states also require a graduate degree. In addition, some states mandate a certain number of hours spent working with children in a supervised counseling setting. School psychologists can work in a traditional public or private school, but they may also work with young people in a variety of other settings, such as juvenile justice centers, community centers, or in a private practice.

Leading the Way: Guidance Counselors

Guidance counselors help students navigate school life in areas such as transitioning from one school to another, applying for summer programs, scheduling classes that best meet their needs, identifying academic and career goals, and applying for college or university. Training for counseling depends on exactly what kind of work you want to do. At minimum, you must earn a bachelor's degree, preferably in psychology, social work, or a related field. If you plan to focus on academic and career counseling, this, along with a state counseling certificate, might be sufficient. However, to help students and their parents deal with social, emotional, and academic challenges, you might need to earn a master's

A guidance counselor helps a student through the college selection and application process using online resources.

degree from a graduate program that specializes in school counseling.

Guidance counselors often do double duty as college counselors. College counselors are just that: they help students make decisions about their college plans, and then they help them achieve their goals. Applying to and being accepted at any institution of higher education can be a daunting task: There are standardized tests to take (e.g., the SAT or ACT), the Common Application and all its many questions and prompts (most colleges and universities use this online site), financial aid forms, transcripts and letters of recommendation, and college essays. These essays are the written works that college applicants include in their file (usually—though not always—within the Common Application itself) to help college admissions directors get to know the students on a more personal level. High school seniors tend to place a lot of stress and anxiety on how to present themselves on the page. Luckily, college counselors are there to give students advice on how to write these essays to maximize their chances of being accepted to the school of their choice. But college counselors aren't just like coaches; some are like sports agents, too. They attend conferences where they meet the admissions directors (the people who make decisions on the university side, whom to accept or reject) and they tour many different schools so that they have first-hand knowledge of the institutions.

CHAPTER FIVE

Like a Boss: Administration and Public Policy

Being involved in education isn't restricted to working in a classroom, or even necessarily in a school. This chapter looks at school governance at the individual school, state, and national levels. Becoming a school administrator and helping shape government education policy work are both "second-order" career options. That is, to do these jobs, you first must have training and experience as a teacher. If you like the idea of networking, fund-raising, public communication, marketing, and management, you might have what it takes to become a principal. If you are attracted to working with the state or national government, consider a career in public policy. These people are involved in the legal side of U.S. education, developing state or national curriculum standards, and creating and administering budgets that determine which schools get how much money from the government.

School Administration

Running a school is very much like running a business. Every institution—corporate or academic—needs at least two things: leadership and money. School leaders help define an educational mission, are the spokespeople for their institutions, and make critical decisions about who works at the school and what kind of programs are available. They also work directly with students, implementing school policies and disciplinary measures. Business managers supervise a school's cash flow, using their training in finance to help the school pay its employees, request government funding, and invest in future projects. Business managers also run the accounting department, which in a public setting keeps track of spending and reimbursement, and in a private school also collects tuition.

Leadership and Curriculum

The head of a school is called the principal (or headmaster in some private schools). Principals are aided by vice or assistant principals. The most effective principals are excellent listeners and communicators. They are responsible for hiring, managing, and evaluating teachers; developing school curriculum; communicating with the department of education or board of directors; and making sure there are enough resources and personnel to ensure a successful school year. Principals know how to build connections within the community, raise funds, and write grants to acquire additional

A principal is the one in charge of discipline and enforcing rules, but he or she can also be a positive role model for young people.

money to improve the physical building(s), add programs such as art, music, or theater, or expand the staff. Principals also act as liaisons with the parent community, broadcasting information about school activities and deadlines. Principals and vice principals are often thought of as disciplinarians, helping write and then enforce school policies. School administrators work long hours and more days than regular faculty and staff. It is a difficult, stressful but highly rewarding job, and to do it, you need advanced degrees and training.

Most administrators start out as classroom teachers. Even in states where teaching experience is not strictly required, it is advantageous—managing teachers and curriculum is much easier if you have been a teacher and have taught the curriculum. So the road to the principal's

Graduating from high school is an important milestone in life.
Teachers and administrators work to enable students to achieve
their highest potential.

office starts with a bachelor's degree, teacher certification, and a few years of teaching experience.

At that point, the aspiring "boss" will need a master's in educational leadership or master's of education (M.Ed.). In these graduate programs, students learn about contemporary educational theory, management techniques, conflict resolution theory, and curriculum development. Once you have earned your graduate degree, you will need further certification in educational leadership. This typically means passing a set of standardized tests. Once you're ready for the job market, you would most likely be hired as an assistant principal first, and then work your way up to principal.

There is a special type of school administrator called the curriculum coordinator. These administrators are not involved in hiring and firing, like principals and heads of schools, but they are very important for shaping what students learn and how they learn it. Being a curriculum coordinator means understanding children's mental, emotional, and physical development from the earliest ages through to young adulthood. They help teachers and other administrators make good decisions about what should be taught in each grade and each subject, and they promote the best methods for teaching based on the research they read. Most curriculum coordinators have master's degrees in curriculum development or have a lot of experience writing curriculum as teachers. "Writing curriculum" is a special kind of writing, not like writing a story or an essay. When you write curriculum, you have to think carefully about the goals and objectives of different lessons and materials, and you have to

EDUCATIONAL TESTING: STATISTICS AND MATH

There is a small but important field of mathematics in education called "psychometrics." This word basically means "measuring mental performance" and it deals with standardized testing and data. This data is important to the department of education—both at the federal and state levels—because they need to answer the question, "Are students learning what we think they should learn?" Standardized testing is the only practical way to answer that question for large numbers of students.

Math experts develop tests (sometimes called "assessments") to measure student achievement.

Psychometrists collect the information, design the tests, and interpret the data using sophisticated computer models. Special graduate degrees in educational psychometrics involve high-level math and sometimes even computer programming. The Educational Testing Service (ETS) is a well-known company that designs and administers educational testing, including the GRE and other common standardized tests. The College Board administers the Scholastic Aptitude Test (SAT) and Advanced Placement (AP) tests, among others. Each state uses its own standards for testing at the elementary and secondary levels. One example of this is New York State's Regents exams, which determine if high school students have achieved the level of performance the state deems sufficient to receive a diploma.

write a clear description of how and what learning should occur. Examples of decisions a curriculum co-ordinator would help make and then describe in some kind of written document are what kind of textbook to purchase for a high school biology classroom, how much homework should be assigned to middle school students, or what physical skills should be emphasized in a school's physical education classes.

Business and Finance

When it comes to the business of running a school, someone needs to manage the costs, income, grants and public subsidies, tuition, and payroll. To do basic accounting work, such as tracking expenses, employees do not need education degrees or advanced training;

An educational business and finance professional combines her knowledge of how schools work with her management skills to keep the school financially healthy.

often an associate's degree in accounting is sufficient. However, a leadership position in school business administration requires many of the same credentials as the job of principal—a bachelor's degree and then a master's degree in educational administration.

Public Policy

The U.S. public school system is massive: more than fifty million primary and secondary students enrolled in fall 2013. Millions more attend universities and colleges funded by the state and federal governments. A career in government can allow you to shape the education system itself. The U.S. Department of Education (DoE) is a relatively small government agency that has one of the largest budgets of any cabinet department. The DoE uses the money in its budget to fund schools and students through grants. It collects data about school performance, promotes national awareness of problems in education that need to be fixed, and attempts to make quality education available to all children. There are a variety of roles in the education area of government: Lawyer, accountant, curriculum specialist, and grant program specialist are some kinds of positions within this government agency. Aside from legal and accounting, which are specialties that have their own degree requirements, you can join the DoE after teaching full-time for only a few years. Graduate degrees are treated favorably but are not required.

The federal government only accounts for about 10 percent of the money that flows through the U.S.

The U.S. Department of Education is a massive organization that oversees the national public school system. It is headquartered in Washington, D.C.

national public school system. Most of that money (more than a *trillion* dollars every year!) comes from state or local sources. That means the tax money individuals and families pay goes to the school systems near where they live. Each state has its own department of education. In turn, local communities decide what to teach students and how to spend the money in their schools. State and local agencies hire people who understand the field of education—people with a degree in education or with experience teaching in the classroom—who can help them set effective policies, determine where money should be spent, and make sure that the money gets to where it needs to go. Although these jobs do not require advanced degrees, you must provide evidence of training in the field of education and be dedicated to improving the public system in your state or community.

CONCLUSION

It would be hard to overstate the profound effect people who work in education can have on individuals, families, communities, nations, and the world. Your career in education will give you the opportunity to be a part of something much larger than yourself. Whether it's a certification; an associate's, bachelor's, or master's degree; or a Ph.D., obtaining the right qualifications for your desired job is essential. What's more, the path there can sometimes be long and take a lot of hard work and focused determination. The good news is that your interest and inspiration mean you're already well on your way.

Although teaching usually comes to mind when we think about a career in education, education is also about learning. This doesn't mean simply learning about an academic subject or how to do a particular job. It also means learning about yourself. Ask serious questions about what kind of person you are, your likes and dislikes, your study and work habits, and what you really want most from life. To get a better idea about who you are, it is absolutely necessary to learn about other people. If you think you might be interested in a career as a teacher, librarian, counselor, school administrator, or government official, seek out people who work in the profession you have in mind. Ask them questions about where they went to school and what degrees or certifications they have. Ask them what they like and dislike about their jobs and what their daily routines are like. Be endlessly inquisitive, and ask them to help. They won't mind. In fact, they love to help.

adjunct professor Professor employed temporarily by a college or university for a specific purpose.

administrator Person who manages a school, college, or university.

associate's degree Two-year degree granted by a community or junior college.

bachelor's degree Degree granted upon completion of an undergraduate program at a college or university.

cognitive development Process of gaining intelligence and advanced thinking and problem-solving skills.

college Institution of higher learning that provides undergraduate courses leading to a bachelor's degree.

community college Low-cost college offering certifications and two-year courses of study; also known as junior college.

curriculum Course of study at the K–12 level, college, or university.

doctorate Doctor of Philosophy; the highest academic degree in many fields of study.

elective Optional or not required.

elementary school School in which instruction is given to children typically in grades pre-K or kindergarten through five or six.

extracurricular Outside the regular course of instruction.

faculty Full-time teaching and administrative staff of a school, college, or university.

funding Supply of money for a purpose such as to run a school.

generalist Person who is trained in many subjects.

graduate level Academic study beyond a bachelor's degree.

interdisciplinary Combining two or more academic disciplines.

master's degree Degree granted by a graduate school upon completion a program of graduate study.

pedagogy The method, principles, or practice of teaching.

public policy Principles by which public education is conceived, managed, and administered.

secondary school Institution in which instruction is given to pre-teens and adolescents, typically in grades six through twelve.

special education Instruction for students who have learning, physical, or emotional needs that cannot be met by the standard school curriculum.

student loan Low-interest loan granted by the federal government, private institutions, schools, colleges, or universities for the purpose of helping students afford a college or university tuition.

teaching certification Certificate stating that the named holder is qualified to teach in public schools.

tenure The right to keep a teaching job for as long as you want to have it.

terminal degree Highest academic degree in a particular field of study.

tuition Fee charged to attend a school.

undergraduate College or university student who has not yet earned a bachelor's degree.

university Institution of learning at the highest level that provides undergraduate and graduate programs.

FOR MORE INFORMATION

American Library Association (ALA)
50 East Huron Street
Chicago, IL 60611
(800) 545-2433
Website: http://www.ala.org
The American Library Association is the oldest and
largest library association in the world, providing
association information, news, events, and
advocacy resources for members, librarians,
and library users.

Association of American Educators
115 South Union Street, Suite 250
Alexandria, VA 22314
(877) 385-6264
Website: http://www.aaeteachers.org
This is the largest national, non-union, professional educators' organization, and it advocates for teachers
and education policies.

Chronicle of Higher Education
1255 Twenty-Third Street NW, 7th Floor
Washington, DC 20037
(202) 466-1000
Website: http://www.chronicle.com
The Chronicle of Higher Education is an online
source of news, information, advice, and jobs
for college and university faculty members and
administrators.

National Association for the Education of Young
    Children (NAEYC)
1313 L Street NW, Suite 500
Washington, DC 20090
(800) 424-2460
Website: http://www.naeyc.org
This professional organization promotes excellence in
    early childhood education by providing information
    for educators and parents, conference informa-
    tion, professional development opportunities and
    resources, and advocating for funding and public
    policy support.

TESOL International Association
1925 Ballenger Avenue, Suite 550
Alexandria, VA 22314
(703) 836-0774
Website: http://www.tesol.org
"TESOL" stands for "Teaching English to Speakers of
    Other Languages." The TESOL International Asso-
    ciation advances professional expertise in English
    language teaching and learning for speakers of
    other languages worldwide.

U.S. Department of Education
400 Maryland Avenue SW
Washington, DC 20202
(800) 872-5327
Website: http://www.ed.gov
The U.S. Department of Education is the central
    source of information on federal funding for

education, public policy in education, news that relates to public education, and information about its many educational initiatives and laws, such as the Common Core State Standards.

Websites

Because of the changing nature of Internet links, Rosen Publishing has developed an online list of websites related to the subject of this book. This site is updated regularly. Please use this link to access this list:

http://www.rosenlinks.com/RDFM/Educ

FOR FURTHER READING

Christen, Carol, and Richard N. Bolles. *What Color Is Your Parachute? For Teens, 2nd Edition: Discovering Yourself, Defining Your Future.* New York, NY: Ten Speed Press, 2010.

Ferguson Publishing. *Coaches and Fitness Professionals* (Ferguson's Careers in Focus). New York, NY: Ferguson Publishing, 2008.

Ferguson Publishing. *Education* (Ferguson's Careers in Focus). 3rd ed. New York, NY: Ferguson Publishing, 2009.

Fiske, Edward B. *The Fiske Guide to Colleges 2014.* New York, NY: Sourcebooks, 2013.

Fourie, Denise K., and David R. Dowell. *Libraries in the Information Age: An Introduction and Career Exploration* (Library and Information Science Text Series). Santa Barbara, CA: Libraries Unlimited, 2009.

Green, Tena. *Your First Year as a Principal, Revised 2nd Edition: Everything You Need to Know That They Don't Teach You in School.* Ocala, FL: Atlantic Publishing Group, 2013.

Griffith, Susan. *Teaching English Abroad 2014: Your Expert Guide to Teaching English Around the World.* 13th ed. London, England: Crimson Publishing, 2014.

Helmes, Jeffrey L., and Daniel T. Rogers. *Majoring in Psychology: Achieving Your Education and Career Goals.* Hoboken, NJ: Wiley-Blackwell, 2011.

Institute for Career Research. *Career as a High School Teacher* (Careers Ebooks). North Charleston, SC: CreateSpace Independent Publishing Platform, 2012.

Institute for Career Research. *Career as a Music Education Teacher* (Careers Ebooks). North Charleston, SC: CreateSpace Independent Publishing Platform, 2012.

Institute for Career Research. *Career as a Teacher— Early Childhood Education* (Careers Ebooks). North Charleston, SC: CreateSpace Independent Publishing Platform, 2013.

Institute for Career Research. *Career as a Teacher— Kindergarten Teaching* (Careers Ebooks). North Charleston, SC: CreateSpace Independent Publishing Platform, 2012.

Institute for Career Research. *Career as a Teacher— Special Education* (Careers Ebooks). North Charleston, SC: CreateSpace Independent Publishing Platform, 2013.

Institute for Career Research. *Career as a Teacher of Theater Arts, Drama Coach* (Careers Ebooks). North Charleston, SC: CreateSpace Independent Publishing Platform, 2013.

Magnuson, Sandy, Robyn S. Hess, and Linda M. Beeler. *Counseling Children and Adolescents in Schools: Practice and Application Guide.* Thousand Oaks, CA: SAGE Publications, 2011.

Martinez, Deirdre. *Washington Internships: How to Get Them and Use Them to Launch Your Public Policy Career.* Philadelphia, PA: University of Pennsylvania Press, 2011.

O'Connell, Dr. Richard P. *The Secrets to Being a Great School Counselor.* North Charleston, SC: CreateSpace Independent Publishing Platform, 2011.

Peterson's. *Teens' Guide to College and Career Planning.* Paramus, NJ: Peterson's, 2011.

Reeves, Diane Lindsey, and Kelly Gunzenhauser. *Career Ideas for Teens in Education and Training* (Career Ideas for Teens). New York, NY: Ferguson Publishing, 2012.

Silivanch, Annalise. *A Career as a Teacher* (Essential Careers). New York, NY: Rosen Publishing, 2010.

Stern, Emily, and Ruth Zealand. *Starting Your Career in Art Education.* New York, NY: Allworth Press, 2013.

BIBLIOGRAPHY

Ayers, William, ed. *To Become a Teacher: Making a Difference in Children's Lives*. New York, NY: Teachers College, 1995.

College Board. "About Us." Retrieved February 1, 2014 (http://www.collegeboard.org/about).

Donaldson, Gordon A., Jr. *How Leaders Learn: Cultivating Capacities for School Improvement*. New York, NY: Teachers College, 2008.

Furr, R. Michael, and Verne R. Bacharach. *Psychometrics: An Introduction*. Thousand Oaks, CA: SAGE, 2013.

Henderson, Anne T., Karen L. Mapp, Vivian R. Johnson, and Don Davies. *Beyond the Bake Sale: The Essential Guide to Family-School Partnerships*. New York, NY: The New Press, 2007.

Learning Express. *Best Careers for Teachers: Making the Most of Your Teaching Degree*. New York, NY: Learning Express, 2010.

National Association for the Education of Young Children. Retrieved February 2, 2014 (http://www.naeyc.org).

New York State Education Department. Retrieved February 2, 2014 (http://www.nysed.gov).

Parkay, Forrest W., and Beverly Hardcastle Standford. *Becoming a Teacher*. 7th ed. New York, NY: Pearson Education, 2007.

Parks, Jerry L. *So, You Want to Become a National Board Certified Teacher Workbook & Evidence Manual*. N.p.: iUniverse, 2012.

Siccone, Frank. *Essential Skills for Effective School Leadership*. Boston, MA: Pearson, 2012.

Smith, Richard E. *Human Resources Administration: A School-Based Perspective*. 4th ed. Larchmont, NY: Eye on Education, 2009.

Starkey, Lauren. *Change Your Career: Teaching as Your New Profession*. New York, NY: Kaplan Publishing, 2007.

Teach.org Coalition, U.S. Department of Education. "Licensing and Certification Requirements." Retrieved January 15, 2014 (https://www.teach.org/teaching-certification).

Wong, Harry K., and Rosemary T. Wong. *The First Days of School: How to Be an Effective Teacher*. Mountain View, CA: Harry K. Wong Publications, 2009.

INDEX

About the Author

Joseph Kampff is a lifelong student of literature with a deep interest in the history of education and current debates over educational policy. He has a bachelor's degree from the New School in New York City, an advanced graduate certificate in cultural studies from Stony Brook University, and a master's in English from Stony Brook University. He lives in Brooklyn, New York, with his family.

Photo Credits

Cover (figure) Dan Kosmayer/Shutterstock.com; cover (background), pp. 4–5 (background) hxdbzxy/Shuttestock.com; back cover, pp. 7, 22, 31 (top), 43, 54 YanLev/Shutterstock.com; p. 1 Andresr/Shutterstock.com; p. 5 Pressmaster/Shutterstock.com; pp. 8–9 bikeriderlondon/Shutterstock.com; pp. 12–13 Digital Vision/Thinkstock; p. 14 Cavan Images/Digital Vision/Getty Images; p 18 courtesy of Thomas Snyder; pp. 20, 24, 36–37 Hill Street Studios/Blend Images/Getty Images; p. 23 Richard Lewisohn/Photodisc/Getty Images; pp. 25, 27, 52, 60 © AP Images; p. 31 Kristian Sekulic/Vetta/Getty Images; p. 33 George Dolgikh/Shutterstock.com; pp. 40–41 Steve Dunwell/The Image Bank/Getty Images; p. 44 Chris Schmidt/E+/Getty Images; p. 46 Jupiterimages/Stockbyte/Thinkstock; p. 49 Dave Buffington/Photodisc/Getty Images; pp. 56–57 © Spencer Grant/PhotoEdit; p. 58 Mike Watson Images/moodboard/Thinkstock; p. 62 Stock4B-RF/Getty Images; p. 64 Saul Loeb/AFP/Getty Images; additional cover and interior design elements PremiumVector/Shutterstock.com, Mike McDonald/Shutterstock.com (emblem components), Milena_Bo/Shutterstock.com, ririro/Shutterstock.com, The_Pixel/Shutterstock.com, Zffoto/Shutterstock.com, Rafal Olechowski/Shutterstock.com (banners, backgrounds).

Designer: Michael Moy; Executive Editor: Hope Lourie Killcoyne; Photo Researcher: Karen Huang